Way Cool

Spanish
Phrase Book

Third Edition

JANE WIGHTWICK

Mc
Graw
Hill
Education

New York Chicago San Francisco Lisbon London Madrid Mexico City
Milan New Delhi San Juan Seoul Singapore Sydney Toronto

About this book

Jane Wightwick
had the idea

Wina Gunn
wrote the pages

Leila & Zeinah Gaafar
(aged 10 and 12) drew the
first pictures in
each chapter

Robert Bowers
(aged 52) drew the other
pictures, and designed
the book

Ana Bremon
did the Spanish stuff

Important things that
must be included

ISBN 978-0-07-180741-8
MHID 0-07-180741-1

e-ISBN 978-0-07-180742-5
e-MHID 0-07-180742-X

McGraw-Hill Education products are available at special quantity
discounts to use as premiums and sales promotions or for use in
corporate training programs. To contact a representative, please
e-mail us at bulksales@mcgraw-hill.com.

This book is printed on acid-free paper.

Printed and bound by Tien Wah Press, Singapore.

*This book features companion audio files available for download.
To access this material, visit McGraw-Hill Professional's Media Center at:
www.mhprofessional.com/mediacenter, then enter this book's ISBN and
your e-mail address. You will receive an e-mail message with a download
link for the additional content. This book's ISBN is: 0-07-180741-1.*

What's inside

Making friends

How to be cool with the group

Wanna play?

Our guide to joining in everything from hide-and-seek to the latest electronic game

Feeling hungry

Order your favorite foods or go local

Looking good

Make sure you keep up with all those essential fashions

Hanging out

At the pool, beach, or theme park — don't miss out on the action

70

Pocket money

Spend it here!

90

Grown-up talk

blah!
blah!
blah!
blah!

If you really, really have to!

100

Extra stuff

All the handy things — numbers, months, time, days of the week

108

Half a step this way

stepfather/stepmother
padrastro/madrastra
👄 padrastro/madrastra

stepbrother/stepsister
hermanastro/hermanastra
👄 airmanastro/airmanastra

half brother/half sister
medio hermano/medio hermana
👄 medyo airmano/
medyo airmana

Hi!
¡Hola!
👄 ola

What's your name?
¿Cómo te llamas?
👄 komo tay yamas

My name's ...
Me llamo ...
👄 may yamo

8

The Spanish put an upside-down question mark before a question, as well as one the right way up at the end. It's the same with exclamation marks.

¿Isn't that weird? ¡You bet!

from Canada
de Canadá
 day canadah

from Ireland
de Irlanda
 day eerlanda

from Scotland
de Escocia
day escosya

from Wales del País de Gales
day pie-yis day gal-les
That means "the land of the Gauls."

from the U.S.
de los Estados Unidos
day los estados ooneedos

from England
de Inglaterra
day eengla-tairra

10

Los SMS

q acs?
qdms cn qn
xa jgar?
m1ml xfa
bye

Bet you're thinking — those Spanish texts don't make sense! But remember: a Spanish "2" is pronounced "dos," the letter "K" is "kay" and "A" is "ah." The Spanish word for "times" as in 2x2 is "por," so "por favor" (please) becomes "xfa." Get it now? … jajaja!

cn (con)
w/

q acs? (¿que haces?)
UOK?

jajaja
LOL

qn (quien?)
who?

xfa (por favor)
plz

qdms (quedamos)
we meetn

xa (para)
4

jgar (jugar)
play

m1ml (mandame un mensaje luego)
txt me

11

How old are you?

¿Cuántos años tienes?

👄 kwantos anyos tee-enes

12 years old

Doce años

👄 dosay anyos

Happy birthday!

¡Cumpleaños feliz!

👄 koomplay-anyos failees

What's your star sign?

¿Qué signo del zodiaco eres?

👄 kay signo del sodee-ako air-res

When's your birthday?

¿Cuándo es tu cumpleaños?

👄 kwando es too koomplay-anyos

Star signs

AQUARIUS

Jan. 21 – Feb. 19
Acuario 👄 akwaree-o

PISCES

Feb. 20 – Mar. 20
Piscis 👄 pees-sees

ARIES

Mar. 21 – Apr. 20
Aries 👄 a-rees

TAURUS

Apr. 21 – May. 21
Tauro 👄 towro

GEMINI

May 22 – June 21
Géminis 👄 hemeenees

CANCER

June 22 – July 23
Cáncer 👄 kansair

LEO

July 24 – Aug. 23
Leo 👄 leo

VIRGO

Aug. 24 – Sep. 23
Virgo 👄 beergo

LIBRA

Sep. 24 – Oct. 23
Libra 👄 leebra

SCORPIO

Oct. 24 – Nov. 22
Escorpio 👄 eskorpee-o

SAGITTARIUS

Nov. 23 – Dec. 21
Sagitario 👄 sa-heetaree-o

CAPRICORN

Dec. 22 – Jan. 20
Capricornio 👄 kapreecornee-o

14

soccer el fútbol
👄 el footbol

rollerblading
el patinaje en línea
👄 el patee-nahay en leenya

music
la música
👄 la mooseeka

electronic games
los juegos electrónicos
👄 los hway-gos elektroneekos

tv
la tele
👄 la taylay

comics
los tebeos
👄 los taybayos

spiders las arañas
👄 las aranyas

school
el colegio
👄 el kòlay-heeyo

15

What's your ...?

¿Cuál es tu ...?

👄 kwal es too ...

favorite group

grupo preferido

👄 groopo prefereedo

favorite color

color preferido

👄 kol-lor prefereedo

Page 69

favorite game

juego preferido

👄 hway-go prefereedo

favorite food

comida preferida

🗨 komeeda prefereeda

favorite ring tone

tono preferido

🗨 tone-oh prefereedo

favorite animal

animal preferido

🗨 anee-mal prefereedo

favorite team

equipo preferido

🗨 ekeepo prefereedo

Talk about your pets

He's hungry
Está hambriento
👄 esta ambree-yento

She's sleeping
Está durmiendo
👄 esta doormee-yendo

Can I pet your dog?
¿Puedo acariciar tu perro?
👄 pwedo asaree-syar
too pair-ro

Do you have
any pets?
¿Tienes alguna
mascota?
👄 tee-enes algoona
mascóta

18

dog

el perro

🗣 el pair-ro

cat

el gato

🗣 el gato

guinea pig

la cobaya

🗣 la kob-eye-a

snake

la serpiente

🗣 la serpee-entay

hamster

el hámster

🗣 el hamstair

parakeet

el periquito

🗣 el peree-keeto

My Little doggy goes *guau guau!*

A Spanish doggy (that's "guauguau" in baby language) doesn't say "woof, woof," it says *"guau, guau"* (*gwa-oo, gwa-oo*). A Spanish bird says *"pío, pío"* (*pee-o, pee-o*) and "cock-a-doodle-do" in Spanish chicken-speak is *"kikirikí"* (*kee-kee ree-kee*). But a cat does say *"miaow"* and a cow *"moo"* whether they're speaking Spanish or English!

music
la música
🫦 la mooseeka

English
el inglés
🫦 el eeng-les

history
la historia
🫦 la eestoreeya

science
las naturales
🫦 las natoorar-les

21

IT
TI
 tay-ee

School rules!

In Spanish-speaking countries many children have to wear a uniform to school and discipline is often strict. On the other hand, they enjoy long vacation breaks: 10 weeks in the summer and another 5–6 during the school year. But before you turn green with envy, you might not like the mounds of *"tareas para las vacaciones"* (*taray-as para las bakasee-yones*), that's "vacation homework"! And if you fail your exams, the teachers could make you repeat the whole year with your little sister!

Gossip

Can you keep a secret?

¿Puedes guardar un secreto?

 pwedes gwardar oon sekreto

Do you have a boyfriend (a girlfriend)?

¿Tienes novio (novia)?

 tee-enes nobyo (nobya)

An OK guy/An OK girl

Un chavo bueno/
Una chava buena

oon chabo bwayno/
oona chaba bwayna

Way bossy!

¡Qué mandón!

 kay man–don

He's/She's nutty!

¡Está como una cabra!

esta komo oona kabra

That means "He's/She's like a goat"!

"I'm not like that at all!"

What a complainer!

¡Qué malasombra!

 kay malas–sombra

You won't make many friends saying this!

Shut up!
¡Cállate!
kigh-yatay

Bug off!
¡Vete a la porra!
betay a la porra

If you're fed up with someone, and you want to say something like "you silly …!" or "you stupid …!", you can start with **"pedazo de"** (which actually means "piece of …") and add anything you like. What about …

Stupid banana!
¡Pedazo de plátano!
(pedaso day platano)

or …

Silly sausage!
¡Pedazo de salchicha! (pedaso day salcheecha)

Take your pick. It should do the trick. You could also try *"¡pedazo de idiota!"* (*pedaso day eedee-ota*). You don't need a translation here, do you?

25

Stop!

¡No hagas eso!

 no agas eso

I want to go home!

¡Me quiero ir a casa!

 may kyairo eer ah kassa

I don't care

Me da igual

 may da eegwal

At last!

¡Por fin!

 por feen

27

Saying goodbye

Here's my address
Aquí tienes mi dirección
👄 akee tee-enes mee
deerek-syon

What's your address?
¿Cuál es tu dirección?
👄 kwal es too deerek-syon

Come to visit me
Ven a visitarme
👄 ben a beesee-tarmay

Have a good trip!
¡Buen viaje!
🫦 bwen bee-ahay

Write to me soon
Escríbeme pronto
🫦 eskree-bemay pronto

Send me a text
Envíame un SMS
🫦 envee-armay oon "SMS"

Let's chat online
¿Chateamos?
🫦 chatay-amos

Bye!
¡Adiós
🫦 adeeyos

What's your email address?
¿Cuál es tu mail?
🫦 kwal es too mail

J□@3◇*@ℛ.com

29

WANNA PLAY?

el elástico

🗣 el elasteeko

el ping-pong

🗣 el "ping-pong"

el reproductor
 el raypro-
dooktor

el yo-yó
 el "yo yo"

el celular
 el saylyoolar

Do you want to play ...?

¿Quieres jugar ...?

👄 keyair-res hoogar

... foos-ball?

... al futbolín?

👄 al footboleen

... cards?

... a las cartas?

👄 a las kartas

... on the computer?

... con el ordenador?

👄 kon el orden-ador

... tic-tac-toe?

... a las tres en raya?

👄 a las trays en righ-ya

33

Fancy a game of **foal** or **donkey**?!

In Spain, you don't play "leap frog," you play "foal" – **el potro**. There is also a group version of this called "donkey" – **el burro**. This involves two teams. Team 1 line up in a row with their heads down in the shape of a donkey. Team 2 take it in turns to leap as far as they can onto the back of the "donkey." If the donkey falls over, Team 2 win. If Team 2 touch the ground or can't leap far enough to get all the team on, then Team 1 win – got that?! Spanish children will try to tell you this is enormous fun, but your parents might not be so keen on the bruises!

Can my friend play too?

¿Mi amigo también puede jugar?

mee ameego tam-byen pway-day hoogar

I have to ask my parents

Se lo tengo que pedir a mis papás

say loe tengo kau pedeer ah mees pa-pas

Make yourself heard

Who dares?

You're it!

¡La quedas tú!

🗣 la kedas too

Race you!

¿Una carrera?

🗣 oona karraira

I'm first

Soy el primero (boys)

Soy la primera (girls)

🗣 soy el preemairo

36 soy la preemaira

37

Electronic games

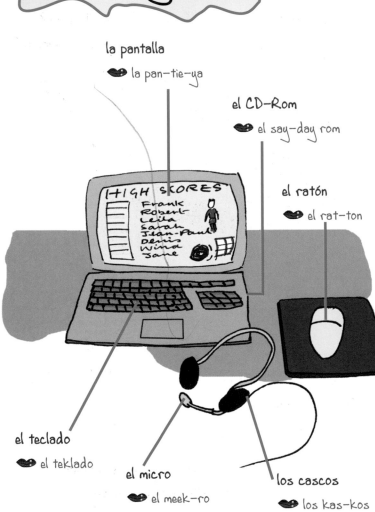

la pantalla
la pan–tie–ya

el CD–Rom
el say–day rom

el ratón
el rat–ton

el teclado
el teklado

el micro
el meek–ro

los cascos
los kas–kos

Show me

Enséñame

 ensay-nyamay

What do I do?

¿Qué hay que hacer?

 kay eye kay asair

Am I dead?

¿Me han matado?

💋 may an matado

Shoot-em-up!

¡Dispárales!

💋 deespar-ralayz

How many lives do I have?

¿Cuántas vidas tengo?

💋 kwantas beedas tengo

How many levels are there?

¿Cuántos niveles hay?

💋 kwantos neebay-les eye

It's virtual fun!

Do you have WiFi?
¿Tienes wifi?

teeyenes weefee

Make sure you say it like this to avoid blank looks!

Send me a message.
Mándame un mensaje.

How do i join?
¿Cómo me apunto?

I'm not old enough.
No tengo edad suficiente.

I'm not allowed.
No tengo permiso.

I don't know who you are.
No te conozco.

my blog
mi blog
👄 mee blog

my friends
mis amigos
👄 mees ameegos

my photos
mis fotos
👄 mees fotos

my videos
mis videos
👄 mees bee-dayos

my music mi música
👄 mee mooseeka

41

Non couch-potato activities!

tennis
el tenis
👄 el tenees

trampolining
el trampolín
👄 el "trampoline"

bowling
los bolos
👄 los bol-los

swimming
la natación
👄 la nata-syon

42

hockey
el hockey
👄 el "hockey"

gymnastics
la gimnasia
👄 la heem-nasya

ballet
el ballet
👄 el ballay

basketball
el baloncesto
👄 el ballon-sesto

and, of course, we haven't forgotten *"el fútbol"*... (P.T.O.) 43

soccer

cleats

las botas

👄 las botas

football gear

el equipo de fútbol

👄 el ekeepo day footbol

ref

el árbitro

👄 el arbeetro

shin-pads

las espinilleras

👄 las espinee-yeras

Good save!

¡Vaya parada!

👄 baya parada

Pass! ¡Pasa!

👄 pasa

45

defender
el defensa
💋 el day-fensa

attacker
el delantero
💋 el daylan-tairo

Foul!
¡Falta!
💋 falta

Penalty!
¡Penalti!
💋 "penalty"

He pushed me!
¡Me ha empujado!
💋 may a empoo-hado

Goal!
¡Gol!
💋 gol

46

Keeping the others in line

Not like that!

¡Así no!

👄 asee no

You cheat! ¡Tramposo! (boys only)

¡Tramposa! (girls only)

👄 tramposo/tramposa

I'm not playing anymore

Ya no juego

👄 ya no hwego

It's not fair!

¡No es justo!

👄 no es hoosto

Stop it!

¡No hagas eso!

👄 no agas eso

Showing off

... do a handstand?

... hacer el pino?

🗨 asair el peeno

Can you ...

¿Sabes ...

🗨 sabays

Look at me!

¡Mírame!

🗨 meera–may

... do a cartwheel?

... dar volteretas laterales?

🗨 dar boltair–retas latairal–le:

... do this?

... hacer esto?

🗨 asair esto

48

Tongue tied

I'd kill for a nice juicy steak!

Impress your Spanish friends with this!

You can show off to your new Spanish-speaking friends by practicing this tongue twister:

Tres tristes tigres comían trigo en un trigal.
trays treestays teegrays comee-an treego en oon treegal
(This means "Three sad tigers ate wheat in a wheat field.")

Then see if they can do as well with this English one:

"She sells seashells on the seashore, but the shells she sells aren't seashells, I'm sure."

49

For a rainy day

deck of cards
una baraja de cartas
👄 oona baraha day kartas

my deal/your deal
yo doy/tú das
👄 yo doy/too das

king
el rey
👄 el ray

queen
la reina
👄 la ray-eena

jack
la jota
👄 la hota

joker
el komodín
👄 el komodeen

tréboles
👄 trebol-les

corazones
👄 korazon-nes

picas
👄 peekas

diamantes
👄 dee-amantau

Do you have the ace of swords?!

You might also see Spanish children playing with a different pack of cards. There are only 48 cards instead of 52 and the suits are also different. Instead of clubs, spades, diamonds and hearts, there are gold coins (**oros**), swords (**espadas**), cups (**copas**) and batons (**bastos**).

chessboard el tablero
🗣 el tablairo

el alfil
🗣 el alfeel

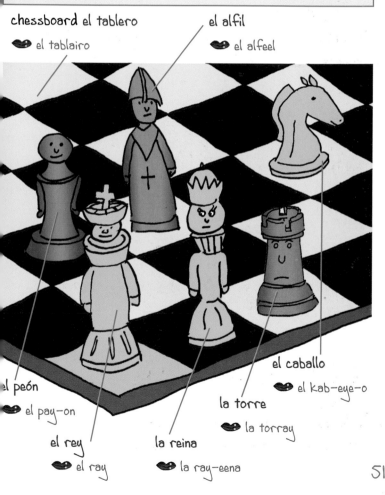

el peón
🗣 el pay-on

el rey
🗣 el ray

la reina
🗣 la ray-eena

la torre
🗣 la torray

el caballo
🗣 el kab-eye-o

F
E
E
L
I
N
G

H
U
N
G
R
Y

hamburger
la hamburguesa
la amboorgaysa

fries
las papas fritas
las papas
freetas

ice cream
el helado
el elardo

Fries

Cola

coke
una coca
oona koka

Grub

I'm starving

Tengo un hambre de lobo

💋 tengo oon ambray day lobo

That means "I have the hunger of a wolf"!

el lobo

Please can I have ...

Por favor, me da ...

💋 por fabor, may da

54

... a croissant

un cruasán

👄 oon krwasan

... a cream pastry

un bollo con nata

👄 oon boyo kon nata

... a sweet roll

una palmera

👄 oona palmayra

... a waffle

un wafle

👄 oon wah-flay

... a muffin

una magdalena

👄 oona magda-layna

los churros

🗣 los choorros

These are wonderful sugary dounut-like snacks. They are sold in cafés and kiosks and usually come in a paper cone. They are also very popular for breakfast in winter, with thick hot chocolate (***chocolate con churros***).

YOU: Can I have some churros, Mom?

Mom: No. They'll make you fat and rot your teeth.

YOU: But I think it's good to experience a foreign culture through authentic local food.

Mom: Oh, all right then.

Churros? *"¡Mm, mm!,"* Garlic sandwich? *"¡Agh!."* If you're going to make foody noises you'll need to know how to do it properly in Spanish! "Yum, yum!" is out in Spanish. You should say *"¡Mm, mm!."* And "Yuk!" is *"¡Agh!"* (pronounced *"ag"*), but be careful not to let adults hear you say this!

... a lemonade

... una limonada

👄 oona leemonadah

I n Mexico and other countries the "limonadas" are carbonated. So instead of a plain lemonade, you're getting a lemon or lime soda-pop.

... water agua

👄 agwa

... a milkshake

... un batido de leche

👄 oon bateedo day lechay

Y ou get your hot chocolate in a large cup (to dunk your churros in).

... a hot chocolate

... un chocolate

👄 oon chokolatay

Are you a hot head?!

If you're travelling in Mexico and Central America and you don't like hot spicy food, a good question to know is "**¿Es picante?**" (*es peekantay* – "Is it spicy?"). If the answer is no, your tongue won't catch on fire!

And if you're hungry for comfort food, you can ask for one of the following dishes:

noodle soup

sopa de fideos

 💋 sopa day feeday-os

spaghetti

espaguetis

💋 espaghetees

... with meatballs

... con albóndigas

💋 kon albon-deegas

and there's always…

pizza

pizza

💋 peesa

Parties

balloon el globo
🗨 el glow-bo

Can I have some more?
¿Me puedes dar más?
🗨 may pwedays dar mas

party hat
el gorro de fiesta
🗨 el gorro day fee-esta

This is for you
Esto es para ti
🗨 esto es para tee

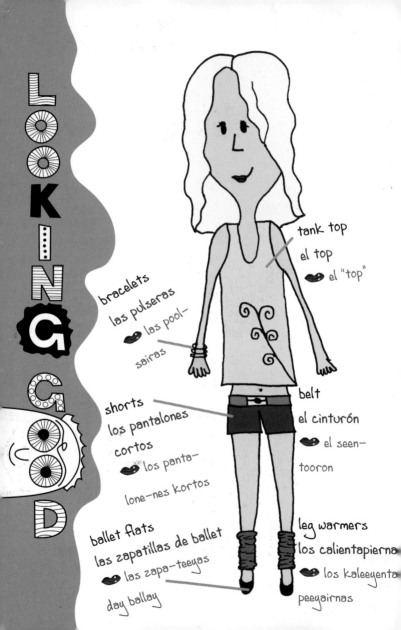

LOOKING GOOD

tank top
el top
👄 el "top"

bracelets
las pulseras
👄 las pool-
saíras

belt
el cinturón
👄 el seen-
tooron

shorts
los pantalones
cortos
👄 los panta-
lone-nes kortos

ballet flats
las zapatillas de ballet
👄 las zapa-teeyas
day ballay

leg warmers
los calientapierna
👄 los kaleeyenta
peeyairnas

Clothes

jeans
los vaqueros
 los bakayros

sweatshirt
la sudadera
la sooda dayra

T-shirt
la camiseta
la kameeseta

soccer jersey
la camiseta de fútbol
la kameeseta day footbo

tennis shoes
las deportivas
las daypor-teebas

shoes
los zapatos
los sapatos

spotted
de lunares
💋 day loonar-res

flowery
de flores
💋 day flor-res

frilly
con volantitos
💋 kon bolanteetos

glittery
con brillos
💋 kon breeyos

striped
de rayas
💋 day righ-yas

67

Make it up!

lip gloss
el brillo de labios
🫦 el breeyo day labyos

glitter gel
la brillantina
🫦 la breeyan-teena

nail polish
el barniz de uñas
🫦 el barnees day oon-yas

earrings los aretes
🫦 los aray-tays

I need a mirror
Necesito un espejo
🫦 netsayseeto oon espay-ho

eye shadow
la sombra de ojos
🫦 la sombray day o-hos

Can you lend me your flat iron?
¿Me prestas tu alisador de pelo?
🫦 may pray-stas too alee-sadoor day pay-lo

68

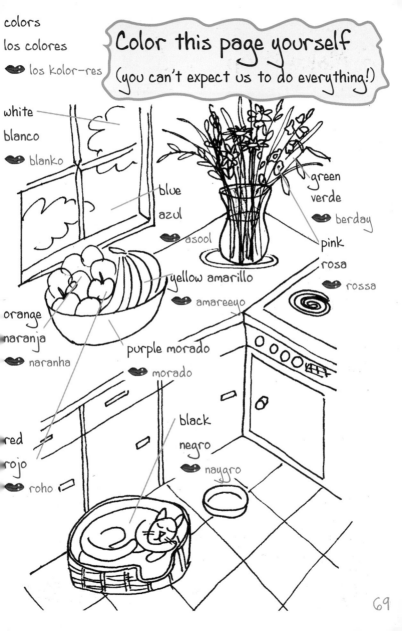

What should we do?

¿Qué hacemos?

👄 kay asay-mos

Can I come?

¿Puedo ir?

👄 pwedo eer

Where do you all hang out?

¿Por dónde salen ustedes?

👄 por donday salen oos-tedays

That's mega!

¡Qué emoción!

👄 kay aymosee-yon

I'm (not) allowed

(No) me dejan

👄 (no) may day-han

Let's go back Regresemos
💋 regray–saymos

That gives me goose bumps (or "chicken flesh" in Spanish!)

Eso me pone la carne de gallina
💋 eso may ponay la karnay day gayeena

I'm bored to death
Me muero de aburrimiento
💋 may mwero day aburree–mee–ento

That's a laugh
Te ríes cantidad
💋 tay reeyes kanteedad

73

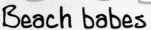

Beach babes

Can I borrow this?

¿Me dejas esto?

👄 may dehas esto

Let's hit the beach

Vamos a la playa

👄 bamos a la playa

Is this your bucket?

¿Es tuyo este cubo?

👄 es tooyo estay koobo

You can bury me

Me puedes enterrar

👄 pay pwedes entair-rar

Stop throwing sand!

¡Deja de echar arena!

👄 dayha day echar arayna

Mind my eyes!

¡Cuidado con mis ojos!

👄 kweedado kon mees ohos

74

sandcastle
el castillo de arena
🗣 el casteeyo day arayna

sea
el mar
🗣 el mar

beach la playa
🗣 la playa

towel
la toalla
🗣 la toe-aya

bathing suit
el bañador
🗣 el banyador

bucket el cubo
🗣 el koobo

snorkel
el tubo
🗣 el toobo

shells
las conchas
🗣 las konchas

shovel
la pala
🗣 la palla

75

It's going swimmingly!

How to make a splash in Spanish!

Let's hit the swimming pool

Vamos a la piscina

👄 bamos a la peeseena

Can you swim (underwater)?

¿Sabes nadar (debajo del agua)? 👄 sabays nadar (debaho del agwa)

Me too/I can't

Yo también/Yo no

👄 yo tambeeyen/ yo no

Can you dive?

¿Te sabes tirar de cabeza?

I'm getting changed

Me estoy cambiando

👄 may estoy kambee-ando

👄 tay sabays teerar day kabaysa

76

Can you swim ...?
¿Sabes nadar ...?
👄 sabays nadar

... backstroke
... de espalda
👄 day espalda

... crawl
... a crol
👄 a krol

... butterfly
... a mariposa
👄 a mareeposa

... breaststroke ... a braza de pecho 👄 a brasa day paycho

slide
el tobogán
👄 el tobogan

goggles
las gafas
👄 las gafas

77

Downtown

Do you know the way?

¿Te sabes el camino?

🗣 tay sabays el kameeno

Let's ask

Vamos a preguntar

🗣 bamos a pray-goontar

Pooper-scoopers on wheels!

In Spain, you might see bright green-and-white motorcycles with funny vacuum cleaners on the side riding around town scooping up the dog poop. The people riding the bikes look like astronauts! (Well, you'd want protection too, wouldn't you?)

bus

el autobús

🗣 el owtoboos

Is it far?

¿Está lejos?

👄 esta lay-hos

Are we allowed in here?

¿Nos dejan entrar aquí?

👄 nos day-han entrar akee

car

el coche

👄 el kochay

You could gain a lot of street cred with your new Spanish-speaking friends by using a bit of slang.
A clapped-out car is *"una cafetera"* (*oona kafaytayra*), which means "coffee pot"! Try this: *"¡Vaya cafetera!"* (*baya kafaytayra* – "What an old clunker!").

79

Park yourself here

swings los columpios
🗨 los koloom-peeyos

jungle gym el juego para escalar 🗨 el hway-go para eska-lar

playground el patio de recreo
🗨 el pateeyo day rekrayo

grass la hierba
🗨 la yairba

tree el árbol
🗨 el ar-bol

slide
el tobogán
🗨 el tobogan

park el parque 🗨 el parkay

Can we play ball games?

¿Podemos jugar a la pelota?

🗣 poday-mos hoo-gar a la pay-lota

roundabout

el carrusel

🗣 el kar-roosel

sandbox

el arenero

🗣 el arain-airo

Can I have a go? ¿Puedo intentarlo?

🗣 pwaydo intain-tarloe

Picnics

I hate wasps

Odio las avispas

🗣 odeeyo las abeespas

Move over!

¡Apártate!

🗣 apar-tatay

bread

el pan 🗣 el pan

Shall we sit here?

¿Nos sentamos aquí?

🗣 nos sentamos akee

napkin

la servilleta

🗣 la serbeeyeta

ham el jamón

🗣 el hamon

cheese

el queso

🗣 el kayso

yogurt
el yogur

🗣 el yogur

chips

las papas fritas

🗣 las papas freetas

drinks

las bebidas

👄 las bebeedas

knife

el cuchillo

👄 el koocheeyo

spoon

la cuchara

👄 la koochara

fork

el tenedor

👄 el tenaydor

wasps

las avispas

👄 las abeespas

bees

las abejas

👄 las abayhas

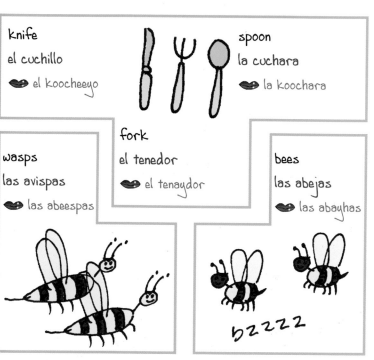

bzzzz

ants

las hormigas

👄 las ormeegas

Wake up, campers!

tent la tienda

🗣 la tyen-da

tent peg
la piqueta

🗣 la pee-kayta

camper van
la caravana

🗣 la kara-vana

penknife
la navaja de bolsillo

🗣 la nava-ha day bol-seelyo

camping stove
el estufa portátil

🗣 el aystoofah porta-teel

sleeping bag el saco de dormir

🗣 el sak-ko day door-meer

flashlight la linterr

🗣 la lintair-na

84

That tent's a palace!
¡Esa tienda es un palacio!
 esa tyen-da es oon palass-yoh

Is there a campfire?
¿Hay una hoguera?
ay oona og-waira

I've lost my flashlight
Perdí mi linterna
pairdee mee lintair-na

These showers are gross
¡Las duchas están sucias!
las doo-chas estan soosyas

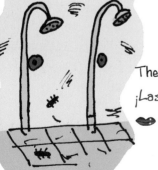

Where does the garbage go?
¿Dónde se tira la basura?
donday say teera la basoora

All the fun of the fair

helter-skelter

el tobogán

🗣 el tobogan

Ferris wheel

la noria

🗣 la noreeya

house of mirrors

la casa de los espejos

🗣 la kasa day los espayhos

bumper cars

los coches de choque

🗣 los kochays

day chokay

Shall we go on this?

¿Nos montamos en éste?

🗣 nos montamos en estay

merry-go-round
el pulpo

👄 el poolpo

It's very fast
Va muy rápido

👄 ba mwee rapeedo

That's for babies
Eso es para los pequeños

👄 eso es para los pekay-nyos

Do you get wet in here?
¿En éste te mojas?

👄 en estay tay mohas

I'm not going on my own
Yo solo no me monto

👄 yo solo no may monto

87

Disco nights

mirror ball
la bola de espejos
💋 la bola day espay-hos

loudspeaker
el altavoz
💋 el altab-os

Can I request a song?
¿Puedo pedir una canción?
💋 pwaydo paydeer oona kan-syon

The music is really lame
¡La música es malísima!
💋 la mooseeka es malee-seema

DJ
el pinchadiscos
💋 el peencha-deeskos

spotlights
los focos
💋 los fo-kos

turntable
el tocadiscos
💋 el toka-deeskos

88

How old do I need to be?

¿Cuántos años hay que tener?

🫦 kwantos anyos ay kay tenair

dance floor

la pista de baile

🫦 la peesta day balay

Let's dance!

¡Vamos a bailar!

🫦 ba-mos a balar

I love this song!

¡Me encanta esta canción!

🫦 may enkanta esta kan-syon

POCKET MONEY

candy
los caramelos
🫦 los karamaylos

T-shirts
las camisetas
🫦 las kameesetas

toys
los juguetes
🫦 los hoogetes

el tendero
🫦 el tendayro

books

los libros

 los leebros

el móvil

 el mobeel

pencils

los lápices

 los lapeeses

What does that sign say?

carnicería

butcher shop

🗣 karneesereeya

pastelería

cake shop

🗣 pasteler
—reeya

panadería

bakery

🗣 panadereeya

confitería

candy store

🗣 confeeter—reeya

papelería

stationers

🗣 papelereeya

verdulería

fruit and vegetable
store

🗣 berdooler—reeya

boutique

clothes shop

🗣 booteek

92

Do you have some cash?

¿Tienes lana?

🗨 tee-enes lanah

I'm broke

No tengo un centavo

🗨 no tengo oon sentahbo

I'm loaded

Estoy forrado

🗨 estoy forrado

Here you go

Aquí tienes

🗨 akee tee-enes

That's a weird shop!

¡Qué tienda más rara!

🗨 kay tyen-da mas ra-ra

That's a bargain Eso es una ganga

🗨 eso es oona ganga

It's a rip-off

Es un robo

🗨 es oon robo

Sweet heaven!

I love this shop

Me encanta esta tienda

💋 may enkanta esta tee-enda

Let's get some candy

Vamos a comprar chucherías

💋 bamos a comprar choochereeyas

Let's get some ice cream

Vamos por un helado

💋 bamos por oon aylado

lollipops

las piruletas

💋 las peerooletas

a bar of chocolate

una tableta de chocolate

💋 oona tableta day chokolatay

chewing gum

el chicle

💋 el cheeklay

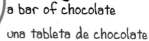

If you really want to look Spanish and end up with lots of fillings, ask for:

regaliz

👄 (regaleez)
soft licorice sticks, available in red or black

polvos pica-pica

👄 (polvos peeka peeka)
tangy fizzy sherbet sold in small packets with a lollipop to dip in

jamones

👄 (hamon-nes)
fruity, fizzy gums in the shape of hams ("ham" is **jamón**)

Chupa-chups®

👄 (choopa-choops)
lollies famous all over the world, but they come from Spain

nubes 👄 (noobes)
soft marshmallow candies ("flumps") in different shades (**nubes** means clouds)

kilométrico

👄 (keelomay-treeko)
chewing gum in a strip like dental floss – pretend to the adults that you're flossing your teeth!

I'm getting ...
Voy a comprar
🗣 boy a comprar

... a pen
... un boli
🗣 oon bolee

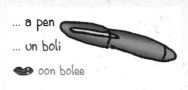

... stamps
... sellos
🗣 seyos

... felt tip pens
... rotuladores
🗣 rotoolador-res

Lápices de colores

... colored pencils
... lápices de colores
🗣 lapeeses day kolor-res

... a key ring
... un llavero
🗣 oon yabairo

... comics
... tebeos
🗣 taybayos

... a fridge magnet

... un imán de nevera

🔊 oon ee-man day nay-baira

... a shell box

... un joyero de conchas

🔊 oon ho-yairo day konchas

... a necklace

un collar

🔊 oon koyar

How much is that?

¿Cuánto cuesta?

🔊 kwanto kwesta

For many years Spain's favorite comics have been *Mortadelo y Filemón*, two accident-prone TIA agents (<u>not</u> CIA) and *Zipi y Zape*, two very naughty twins. Children also like to read *Mafalda*, an Argentinian comic, *Carlitos y Snoopy* (Charlie Brown & Snoopy), *Tintin*, *Astérix* and *¿Dónde está Wally?* (Where's Wally?).

Money talks

How much pocket money do you get?

¿Cuánto te dan para gastos?

💋 kwanto tay dan para gastos

I only have this much

Sólo tengo esto

💋 soul-lo tain-go esto

Can you lend me
ten pesos?

¿Me prestas diez
pesos?

💋 may praystas
deeyes paysos

No way!

¡Ni hablar!

💋 nee ablar

Money talk

Money varies in the different Spanish-speaking countries:

Spain = **euro** (*ay-ooro*)

Mexico = **peso** (*paysoh*)

Guatemala = **quetzales** (*ketsalays*)

Costa Rica = **colones** (*kolonays*)

But if you're in Puerto Rico, you're all set – the money
is U.S. dollars!

GROWN UP TALK

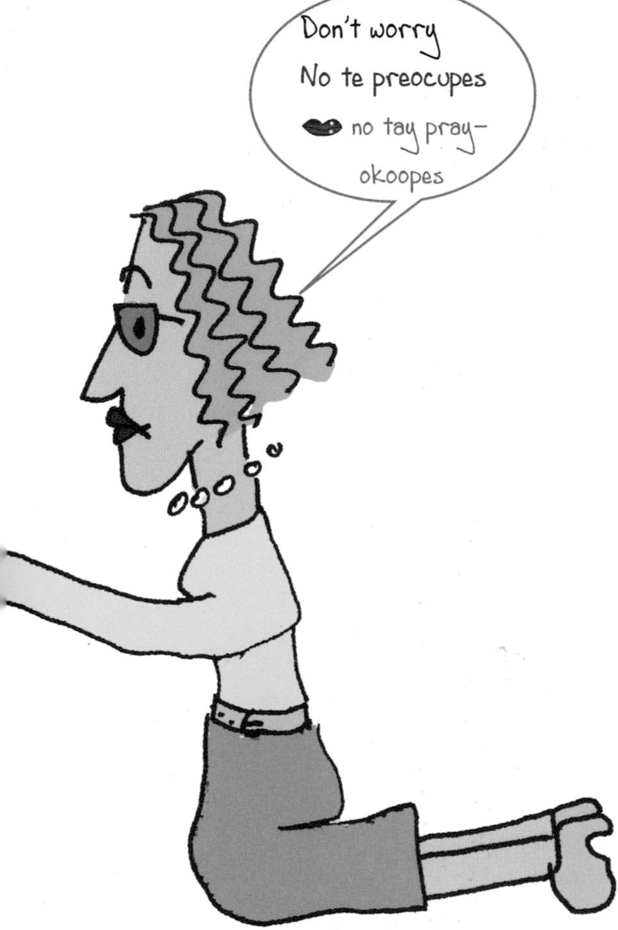

grown-up

adulto

adoolto

Help!

Something has dropped/broken

Algo se ha caído/roto

 algo say a kigh-eedo/roto

Please

Por favor

por fabor

Can you help me?

¿Me puedes ayudar?

 may pwedes ayoodar

Where's the mailbox?

¿Dónde está el buzón?

donday esta el booson

Where are the toilets?

¿Dónde están los aseos?

102 donday estan los asayos

I can't manage it

No puedo

🔴 no pwedo

Could you pass me that?

¿Me pasas eso?

🔴 may pasas eso

What time is it?

¿Qué hora es?

🔴 kay ora es

Come and see

Ven a ver

🔴 ben a bair

May I look at your watch?

¿Me deja que mire su reloj?

🔴 may deha kay meera soo reloh

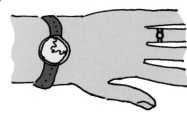

Lost for words

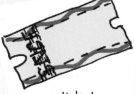

... my ticket
mi billete

👄 mee beeyaytay

I've lost ...
He perdido ...

👄 eh perdeedo

... my cell
phone
mi celular

👄 mee
saylyoolar

... my parents
mis padres

👄 mees padrays

... my shoes
mis zapatos

🗣 mees sapatos

... my money mi dinero

🗣 mee deenayro

... my sweater
mi suéter

🗣 mee sweatair

... my watch
mi reloj

🗣 mee reloh

... my jacket mi chaqueta

🗣 mee chakayta

105

Adults only!

Show this page to adults who can't seem to make themselves clear (it happens). They will point to a phrase, you read what they mean, and you should all understand each other perfectly.

No te preocupes
Don't worry

Siéntate aquí
Sit down here

¿Tu nombre y apellidos?
What's your name and surname?

¿Cuántos años tienes?
How old are you?

¿De dónde eres?
Where are you from?

¿Dónde te alojas?
Where are you staying?

¿Dónde te duele?
Where does it hurt?

¿Eres alérgico a algo?
Are you allergic to anything?

Está prohibido
It's forbidden

Tiene que acompañarte un adulto
You have to have an adult with you

Voy por alguien que hable inglés
I'll get someone who speaks English

weather
el tiempo
 el tyem-po

numbers los números los noo-mairos

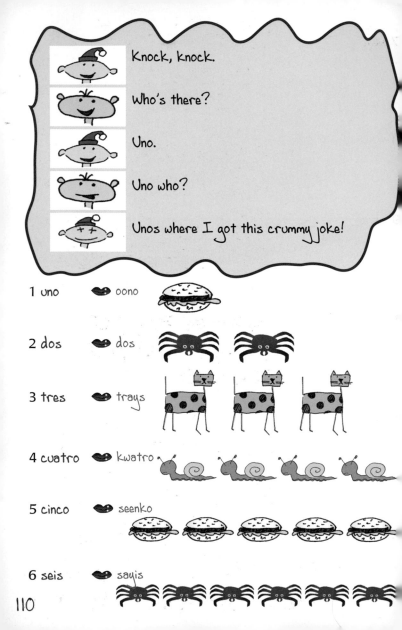

7 siete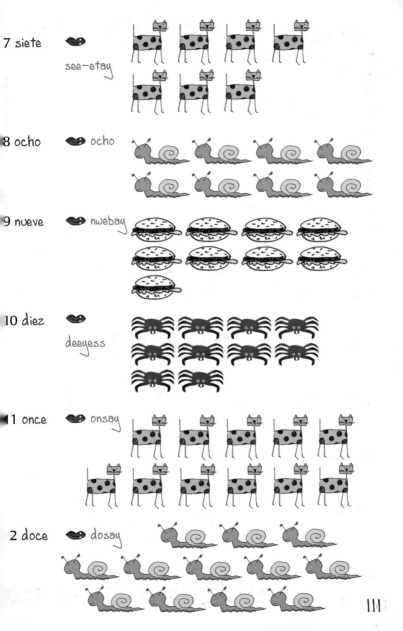
see-etay

8 ocho   ocho

9 nueve   nwebay

10 diez
deeyess

11 once   onsay

2 doce   dosay

111

13 trece  tresay

14 catorce  katorsay

15 quince  keensay

16	dieciséis	*deeyesee sayis*
17	diecisiete	*deeyesee see-etay*
18	dieciocho	*deeyesee ocho*
19	diecinueve	*deeyesee nwebay*

I f you want to say "thirty-two," "fifty-four," and so on, you can just put the two numbers together like you do in English. But don't forget to add the word for "and" (**y**, pronounced *ee*) in the middle:

32	treinta y dos	*traynta ee dos*
54	cincuenta y cuatro	*seenkwenta ee kwatro*
81	ochenta y uno	*ochenta ee oono*

20	viente	*baintay*
30	treinta	*traynta*
40	cuarenta	*kwarenta*
50	cincuenta	*seenkwenta*
60	sesenta	*saysenta*
70	setenta	*saytenta*
80	ochenta	*ochenta*
90	noventa	*nobenta*
100	cien	*seeyen*

a thousand mil *meel*

a million un millón *oon meel-yon*

a gazillion! ¡chorrocientos! *chorroh-seeyentos*

1st	primero	*preemairo*
2nd	segundo	*segoondo*
3rd	tercero	*tersayro*
4th	cuarto	*kwarto*
5th	quinto	*keento*
6th	sexto	*sexto*
7th	séptimo	*septeemo*
8th	octavo	*octabo*
9th	noveno	*nobayno*
10th	décimo	*dayseemo*

Fancy a date?

If you want to say a date in Spanish, you don't need to use 1st, 2nd, etc. Just say the ordinary number followed by *de* (*day*):

Lunes	Martes	Miércoles	Jueves	Viernes	Sábado	Domingo
		1	2	3	4	5
6	7	8	9	10	11	12
13	14	15	16	17	18	19
20	21	22	23	24	25	26
27	28	29	30			

uno de marzo   (1st of March)

diez de julio   (10th of July)

March	marzo	*marso*
April	abril	*abreel*
May	mayo	*my-yo*

June	junio	*hooneeyo*
July	julio	*hooleeyo*
August	agosto	*agosto*

September	septiembre	*septee-embray*
October	octubre	*octoobray*
November	noviembre	*nobee-embray*

December	diciembre	*deesee-embray*
January	enero	*enayro*
February	febrero	*febrayro*

117

primavera   *preemabayra*

SPRING

verano   *berano*

SUMMER

otoño   *otonyo*

AUTUMN

invierno   *eenbee-erno*

WINTER

Monday	lunes	*loon-nes*
Tuesday	martes	*mar-tes*
Wednesday	miércoles	*mee-erkol-les*
Thursday	jueves	*hoo-ebes*
Friday	viernes	*bee-er-nes*
Saturday	sábado	*sabado*
Sunday	domingo	*domeengo*

By the way, many kids have a two-and-a-half hour lunch break! Time enough for lunch and a siesta. But school doesn't finish until 5pm.

Good times

It's ...
Son ...
💋 sonn

(five) o'clock
las (cinco)
💋 las (seenko)

quarter after (two)
las (dos) y cuarto
💋 las (dos) ee kwarto

quarter to (four)
las (cuatro) menos cuarto
💋 las (kwatro) menos kwarto

half past (three)
las (tres) y media
💋 las (trays) ee medya

five after (ten)

las (diez) y cinco

 las (deeyes) ee seenko

twenty after (eleven)

las (once) y viente

 las (onsay) ee baintay

ten to (four)

las (cuatro) menos diez

 las (kwatro) menos deeyes

twenty to (six)

las (seis) menos veinte

 las (sayis) menos baintay

W atch out for "one o'clock." It's a little different from the other times. If you want to say "It's one o'clock" you have to say **Es la una** (*es la oona*). "It's half past one" is **Es la una y media** (*es la oona ee medya*), and so on.

morning

mañana

 la manyarna

midday

mediodía

 el medyo-deeya

afternoon

la tarde

 la tarday

midnight

la medianoche

 la medya-nochay

evening la noche

 la nochay

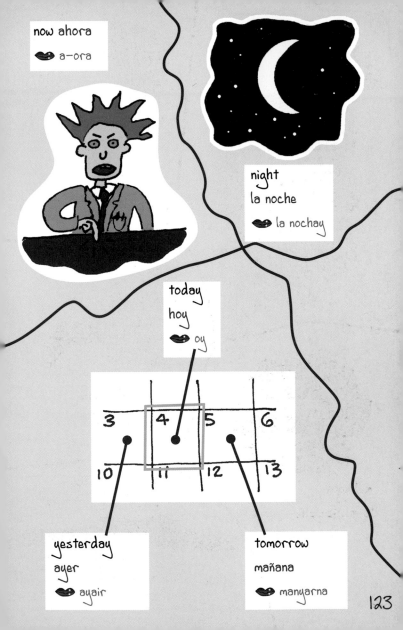

Weather wise

Can we go out?

¿Podemos salir fuera?

👄 podaymos saleer fwera

It's hot

Hace calor

👄 asay kalor

It's cold

Hace frío

👄 asay freeyo

It's horrible

Hace un día horrible

👄 asay oon deeya orreeblay

It's raining seas!

In Spanish it doesn't rain "cats and dogs," it rains "seas"! That's what they say when it's raining really heavily:

¡Está lloviendo a mares!
esta yobeeyendo a mar-res

124

It's windy
Hace viento
👄 asay beeyento

It's sunny
Hace sol
👄 asay sol

It's raining
Está lloviendo
👄 esta yobeeyendo

It's snowing
Está nevando
👄 esta nebando

I'm soaked
Estoy empapado
👄 estoy empapardo

It's nice Hace bueno
👄 asay bweno

125

Signs of life

altura mínima
minimum Height

Móviles
prohibidos
No cell phones

Entrada prohibida
No entry

Sólo mayores
de 18
Over 18s only

Sólo menores de 5
Under 5s only

NO FUNCIONA

OUT OF ORDER

PRIVATE

Privado

Caballeros

Señoras

128